# ICE CREAM

*written by*
H. I. Peeples

*illustrated by*
David Garner

A CALICO BOOK
Published by Contemporary Books, Inc.
CHICAGO · NEW YORK

A Calico Book
Published by Contemporary Books, Inc.
180 North Michigan Avenue, Chicago, Illinois 60601
Copyright © 1988 by The Kipling Press
Text Copyright © 1988 by Robert Cwiklik & Russell Shorto
Illustrations Copyright © 1988 by David Garner
All Rights Reserved.

Art Direction by Tilman Reitzle
Library of Congress Catalog Card Number: 88-17761
International Standard Book Number: 0-8092-4466-7
Manufactured in the United States of America

Published simultaneously in Canada by Beaverbooks, Ltd.
195 Allstate Parkway, Valleywood Business Park
Markham, Ontario L3R 4T8 Canada

Say, that's a fine looking ice cream cone you have there. It looks delicious. But wait! Don't eat it just yet. I've got a thing or two to tell you about your ice cream. Have you ever wondered where it came from? How it was made? Just hold your cone for a few minutes and I'll tell you.

Here is where your ice cream begins—on the farm. It comes from cow's milk. All kinds of cows give milk. But some is richer and creamier, and that's better for ice cream.

Dairy farmers tend their cows carefully, making sure they are healthy and happy. An unhappy cow won't give much milk. The farmers milk the cows twice a day.

Most milk is for people to drink, but some is sent in large trucks to the ice cream plant.

When the milk arrives it is poured into a machine called a separator. This separates the thick part of the milk— the cream—from the rest. Then the milk and cream flow through different pipes into the pasteurizer. This cleans the milk by heating it up to destroy any harmful bacteria.

The cream and milk are mixed together again and stabilizers and emulsifiers are added. These chemicals make the mixture creamier and smoother so that it will make perfect ice cream.

When the temperature reaches 120 degrees (that's hot!), sugar is added.

Now the hot, runny mix flows into another big machine called the homogenizer. This makes the little globules of fat in the mix smaller and spreads them evenly. Otherwise, the fat might turn into butter. Then you'd have an ice butter cone.

Now it's time for this hot stuff to start cooling down. Off it flows into the cooler. Here it relaxes for a few hours. It gets chilled to about forty degrees.

Then the mix is pumped into the freezer. Here it gets squeezed into a very cold tube. This tube is so cold that it freezes the mix in a snap. While this is happening, blades inside the tube are spinning around like a fan. These blades whip the mix to make it nice and light. Otherwise it would be a big lump of ice.

Now we have ice cream!

But there's something missing...it has no flavor! So from the freezer, the ice cream is squeezed into another tube where it mixes with flavors, fruits, nuts —whatever you like. Every company has its own secret recipes for the flavors and these are kept under lock and key.

Now comes the person with the most important job of all—and the best. She is the quality control checker, and her job is to taste each kind of ice cream to make sure it is perfectly creamy, perfectly cold, and perfectly delicious!

When the taster is satisfied, the ice cream gets squirted out into packages. The packages roll along on the assembly line and each one stops for a moment under the hose. Whish! The containers are filled instantly.

The packages go into a deep freeze room, where they are stored until they are to be sold. In here it is *REALLY* cold: about twenty degrees below zero. The people who work in here have to wear lots of warm clothing. When the ice cream has to be delivered…

...it is loaded onto special trucks. These trucks are like freezers on wheels and they keep the ice cream from melting.

Meanwhile, on a hot day at the ice cream parlor, the manager calls the dairy company. "We need more ice cream!" he says. "We're all out of chocolate chip. And you'd better send us some vanilla too."

It doesn't take long for the ice cream truck to arrive.

You can buy ice cream almost anywhere and in all sorts of different sizes. At the ice cream parlor you can buy it by the scoop.

In the supermarket you can buy it by the pint, the quart, or the half-gallon. But no matter where you buy it, and no matter what flavor it is, the best ice cream always come from the same place: cows!

So the next time you see a cow, tell her, "Thanks for the ice cream!"

Okay, that's all! I'm finished.
Now you can eat your...Oh my
gosh! I'm so sorry. I didn't
realize my story had taken so
long.
Well, you'll just have to go
back and get some more!

ABOUT
THE
ARTIST

David Garner is a busy illlustrator living and working in New York City. He is a graduate of the Cooper Union For The Advancement of Science and Art and shows a preference for vanilla–peanut butter ice cream.